M000020594

anchoredman

Five words that could save your life

jason graves

On Belay ob Publishing

Carlsbad, California, U.S.A.
anchoredman.com

Scott-
Stay Tied in!

John 15

Published in Carlsbad, California by On Belay Publishing.

Cover design and illustrations by Ryer Flaker.
Editing by Lynette Trier and Dick Scott.

ISBN 978-0-9831880-0-1

Printed in the U.S.A.

WARNING

Rock climbing is inherently dangerous and could result in serious injury or death. This book is not intended to provide instructions for actual climbing, and only uses rock climbing stories and systems as an illustration for teaching life lessons. The author of this book is not a certified climbing instructor and assumes no liability for accidents happening to, or injuries sustained by, readers of this book. If you have an interest in learning to climb, you should seek training from a certified rock-climbing guide or instructor before attempting any type of climbing.

Contents

Did I Just Kill My Own Son?

"This can't be happening!
God please help me.
Give me the strength for this.
This can't be happening!"
Over and over these words raced through
my mind as I strained to pull the rope up over the
edge of the cliff. My heart was pounding. My mind
was spinning. I was praying that my eight-year-old
son, Cameron, was still alive on the other end. From
the bottom of the cliff, his older brother, Benjamin,
was desperately signaling S.O.S. over and over. I'll
never forget the piercing sound of his plastic whistle
echoing off the canyon walls, rising from one hundred
and seventy feet below. I can still hear the haunting
shriek:

Brrrrt - Brrrrt - Brrrrt!
Brrrrt - Brrrrt - Brrrrt!
Brrrrt - Brrrrt - Brrrrt!

Let me back up. It was the week after Easter,
and I had planned another "Graves boys' adventure"
for my sons Benjamin and Cameron, who were ten and
eight years old. We had just navigated the demanding
schedule of Easter season at church, and I was ready
to get lost in the wild for a few days. I had heard about
some spectacular waterfalls and swimming holes only
an hour north of Los Angeles. Our destination was Tar

Creek, which cascaded through a rugged canyon in a remote area of southern California's Sespe Wilderness.

As a boy, I treasured the times when my father would take my brothers and me to a nearby swimming hole. I was drawn to the exhilaration of balancing on the side of a rock cliff, staring down at the dark waters below – a barefoot, shirtless kid, carefree as a bird, ready to take to the air. After summoning the courage to launch from my perch, I would soar for a few heart-stopping moments, then splash! Now, as a dad, I couldn't wait to pass this important "life skill" on to my boys over the next few sun-filled days.

We loaded up our packs with provisions for three days, which included a 200-foot rope and enough rock climbing equipment to build an anchor. While descending through Tar Creek Canyon, we would need to rappel down two waterfalls, which was no problem for us since I had been teaching Ben and Cam to rock climb and rappel over the past couple of years.

With the exception of my wife, we all had big grins on our faces as the minivan bumped along the dirt almost-road that wound its way through the mountains to the trailhead. Before we waved goodbye, I went over the plans with her one more time:

"The boys and I will hike down Tar Creek Canyon until it meets up with the Sespe River. In

three days, we'll follow the river back to the main road and meet you by noon. If we're not there on time, don't panic. That means we had to hike back another way because the water levels were too high to cross. If we're more than two hours late, you can send help – but that's not going to happen."

Since there was no cell phone coverage, I printed out a map and itinerary that she could give to a rescuer in case of an emergency. It's not the most reassuring thing to discuss right before you take your wife's "little babies" into the backcountry, but I wanted to take every precaution. We snapped a photo with mom, and then wandered off into what would become our most epic adventure to date.

As we explored the creek, it was even better than we had imagined. We caught a water snake, splashed down a natural rock waterslide, and then warmed ourselves by firelight as the golden southern California sun dipped behind the mountains. We talked fearlessly about bears and mountain lions while we filled our bellies with our favorite backpacking dinner: chili and cheese poured into a bag of Fritos corn chips. We were three undomesticated adventurers, completely at home in this rugged habitat.

Tar Creek Canyon

Cameron going over the edge of the first waterfall.

The Point of No Return

The next morning we woke up with the sun, packed up, and headed out. We quickly reached the first waterfall - a seventy-foot plunge into what looked like a miniature version of the Grand Canyon. We rehearsed our plans as I built a rappel anchor near the edge of the cliff.

"Ben, I'll lower you first. When you reach the bottom, blow the whistle once to signal that you are untied from the rope. Then attach the harness and helmet to the rope and blow your whistle two times. That's the signal for me to pull the rope back up. Next, I'll lower Cam, then our backpacks, and lastly, I'll rappel down. If something goes wrong, or you need help, blow the whistle three times."

We created these signals because it would be hard to communicate over the roaring sound of water exploding at the bottom of the falls.

After lots of ecstatic "woo-hoos" echoing through the ravine, we were all safely at the bottom. We were also at the point of no return. Once we dropped into the bowels of Tar Creek Canyon, the only way out was to keep going down. Over the next half mile of treacherous terrain, the creek descends nearly 1200 feet, leading down to a magnificent 170-foot waterfall.

We spent the whole afternoon climbing under, over, and around house-sized boulders. When there was no way around, we wrapped our packs in black garbage bags and floated them across chilly pools.

I Think We're in Over Our Heads

By the time we reached the top of the biggest waterfall, the sun was low on the horizon. I cautiously tiptoed toward the edge. Gulp! As I peeked over, I got that queasy feeling you get if you lean over the railing on the balcony of a high-rise hotel. My boys were used to being lowered by rope after a 50-foot rock climb, but rappelling over a waterfall the height of a 17-story building was something that made all three of us want to click our hiking boots together and say, "There's no place like home."

Now I know what you're thinking – "What kind of dad puts his kids through this?" The short answer is – an ignorant one. But we'll get to that later. To be honest, I didn't really worry about this last rappel until I was actually laying on my belly peeking over the edge. In my head, I know that a fall from 170 feet isn't much different than a fall from 50 feet. However, that logic doesn't mean much when you are gripping the rope backing up toward the precipice. Even though we were more-than-a-little nervous, we knew that we couldn't go back the way we came. It was either face our fears or wait for a helicopter to rescue us.

We had already rappelled once that day, so we had our system down. I put Ben's harness on, said a quick prayer, and began lowering him to the right of where the water plunged over the edge. It took a few minutes for him to reach the ground because I lowered him at a slow, steady pace. Once he touched down and unweighted the rope, I noticed that there was still about 30 feet of leftover rope coiled next to me at the top. This was exactly what I expected since my rope was 200 feet long.

A few more minutes passed, and then I heard Ben blow his whistle once. He had made it down safely. After two more blows, I began dragging the gear back up for round two. I was feeling better since we had overcome our fears and seemed to have conquered the big falls.

Now it was Cameron's turn. We got his harness on and, as usual, I double-checked everything. Cam is my fearless one, so it didn't surprise me that he had a huge grin on his face. I watched his matted, unwashed blonde hair disappear over the cliff as I slowly lowered him. Several minutes passed, and then something peculiar happened, something that both startled and confused me.

As I was feeding rope through my belay device, I noticed there wasn't the appropriate feeling of weight on the other end of the rope. It didn't seem like Cam had been lowering long enough to reach the bottom, so I glanced over at the rope pile. Right away I could see that there was much more than 30 feet of rope still coiled next to me. This meant that my son had not reached the bottom, yet I couldn't feel his weight on the rope anymore.

My heart started racing as I struggled not to panic. I immediately felt sick in the pit in my stomach, which even now revisits me as I tell this story. Then I heard the sound I feared the most: Ben started blowing his whistle in bursts of three. I could sense his terror through its high-pitched shriek. Instinctively, I starting pulling the rope back up but it wouldn't budge.

Cameron only weighed 70 pounds soaking wet, so I thought that if I pulled hard enough I could just drag him up. I pulled with all my might, but the rope seemed hopelessly stuck. I was stumped. I looked over the edge but couldn't see anything because the bottom part of the cliff cut back in like a cave.

I yelled at the top of my voice, "*Benjamin! Where is Cam? I can't see him! What's going on?*"

Did I just kill my own son?

He couldn't hear my voice over the sound of the waterfall. He just kept blowing the whistle over and over in desperation.

My mind raced to the worst. I thought to myself, *Ben's blowing his whistle because he can see that Cameron was crushed by a falling rock. Maybe he's bleeding and unconscious, just dangling in the air. Or maybe he has come off the end of the rope and fallen to his death.*

Oh God, I've killed my own son!

As a last resort, I was prepared to tie off the rope and rappel down myself to see what happened but first, I decided to give the rope one more tug. I prayed for God to give me strength and then pulled with all of my might. This time I felt the rope give a little. *"Yes!"* I pulled again. *"Yes! Yes!"*

I locked the rope off with my belay device and used my legs to push back from the edge. Then, I walked forward as I pulled on the rope. I was dragging Cam up like a deep-sea fisherman reeling in a giant marlin – only there wasn't any movement on the other end of the line. There was weight on the rope, but it felt like I was dragging up a lifeless mass. I just kept praying that Cam would be alive on the other end.

As I pulled for what seemed like an eternity, my arms were burning and my legs were shaking with fatigue. I was out of breath and running out of strength. My mouth was so dry I could hardly form words, but I kept praying out loud for God to help me.

And then the most wonderful thing happened! I felt something on the rope that brought me inexpressible joy. Even though I couldn't see him - and it's hard to explain unless you've spent time belaying a rock climber - I could tell, just by the feel of the rope, that the little bugger was climbing back up the cliff. I started laughing out loud while tears poured down my face.

Within a couple of minutes, I saw my precious boy pull himself over the top – with hardly a scratch on him! He ran over to me and we both started sobbing. I squeezed him so hard his eyeballs almost popped out. After the most terrifying twenty minutes of my life, I could breathe again. My son was alive!

Later that night, Cam explained to me what had happened. Apparently, he started veering toward the waterfall on his descent and grabbed on to a small ledge on the cliff so he wouldn't go into the water. This is why I didn't feel his weight on the rope. As the slack in the rope blew around above him, it must have gotten stuck in a crack. I'm still not sure exactly what happened. What I am sure of is that it was the last time I'd ever put my kids on a rope and hang them off of the side of a cliff.

Cameron and Benjamin at the bottom of the waterfall.

Ventura Search and Rescue helicopter looking for us.

The rest of the trip was relatively uneventful except for one little thing: we didn't reach the rendezvous spot on time. This prompted my incredibly patient, not to mention exceedingly forgiving, wife to alert Ventura County Search and Rescue to look for us. Long story short: we enjoyed a thrilling helicopter ride back into town, which was great fun until I saw the look on her face through the window. Did I mention how patient and forgiving my wife is? After a tearful reunion, we celebrated our safe return over In-N-Out burgers and milkshakes.

For months after our Tar Creek adventure, I was haunted by the memory of almost losing my son. I still get choked up when I think about it. It's too painful to imagine what would have happened if I hadn't been able to pull him back up safely. In retrospect, I realize that my son could have lost his life for one painfully obvious reason – his father was ignorant.

Ignorant: adj; lacking knowledge, unaware

Ignorant. No guy likes to admit it, but that's exactly what I was. I had never been down Tar Creek Canyon before. I was unaware of how treacherous the terrain was. There were important questions with life-and-death consequences that I didn't even know to ask:

"What was the landing like at the bottom of the falls?"

"What would I do if the rope became stuck and I couldn't free it?"

So many things could have gone wrong, and I had no way to call for help. I put what was most important to me at risk due to my ignorance.

It is rare that a week goes by when I don't meet a guy who has lost something precious to him as a result of ignorance. Because I'm a pastor, I see it all the time: A well-meaning guy who, due to some bad habits or temptation, has shattered his marriage, destroyed his family, or lost his job because he didn't know how to protect the things that were most important to him. I'm not talking about jerks, perverts, or overgrown frat boys who are always daydreaming about their next weekend partying in Vegas. I'm talking about guys who are trying to live good lives – guys who want to be men of integrity and character, yet find themselves doing things that will eventually shipwreck their lives.

If you're a guy, you can probably relate to **Romans 7:15 "I don't really understand myself, for I want to do what is right, but I don't do it. Instead, I do what I hate."** *(NLT)* Like many men, you find yourself doing things that you know will screw up your life, but you can't seem to stop. There's a simple proverb from the Bible that I believe can help you with this dilemma. It's so simple that you might dismiss it as basic common sense. Unfortunately, I've found that it is painfully *un*common sense. Ready? Here it is:

Proverbs 22:3 "A prudent person sees trouble coming and ducks; a simpleton walks in blindly and is clobbered." *(The Message)*

Too many guys have been clobbered by some kind of sin because they didn't see it coming. And if they did, they didn't duck! If you're like me, you want to be the kind of guy that a woman, a family, and most importantly, God, can trust. The people you love need you to be that guy. And no matter how messed up you think your life is, you can still be that guy. First, you need to learn to see trouble coming so that you can duck. You have to overcome your lack of knowledge and your unawareness, and replace ignorance with vigilance.

Building a "Bomber" Anchor

Because of the life-and-death nature of rock climbing, there are many skills and safety systems you have to learn before venturing into the vertical world. One of the first skills you learn is how to build an anchor on the side of a cliff. This anchor must be strong enough to hold the extreme force of a falling climber so that he doesn't hit the ground. Climbers have a slang term to describe this kind of anchor: *bomber.*

Bomber

Bomber: adjective; short for "bomb-proof," a term used to describe an anchor or piece of gear that will not fail under extreme loads.

Example:
Climber #1: Why are your legs shaking like Elvis on Red Bull?
Climber #2: I'm about to fall!
Climber #1: Relax, your anchor is bomber.

Commercial airline pilots have a pre-flight checklist they go over in painstaking detail before they get airborne, hit autopilot, and take a nap. Many climbers also go through a mental checklist while constructing an anchor. I've memorized an acronym that takes me through a checklist to remind me of these five words: **Solid, Redundant, Equalized,** and **No Extension.** Before I clip into an anchor, I always ask myself, "Is this anchor **S.R.E.N.E.?**" If I'm going to literally bet my life - not to mention my wife's husband and my kids' dad - on this anchor, I want to be sure that it's bomber.

In the next four chapters of this book, I'm going to teach you the **S.R.E.N.E.** system for building a rock-climbing anchor. From this acronym, you'll learn how these five words can literally save your life. You'll also discover a realistic, step-by-step plan for becoming the leader and protector God created you to be. It's a practical system for staying anchored to God that has worked in my life. It won't be easy, but it's very doable.

Maybe you think rock climbers are nut-jobs with a death wish. Maybe you get dizzy standing halfway up a ladder. Even if you never find yourself dangling from the side of a cliff, you'll be glad you know about **S.R.E.N.E.!**

Action Step: *Before starting chapter two go to the **"tools"** section at **anchoredman.com** and watch the instructional video on how to build a rock-climbing anchor. It will make the rest of this book much easier to understand!*

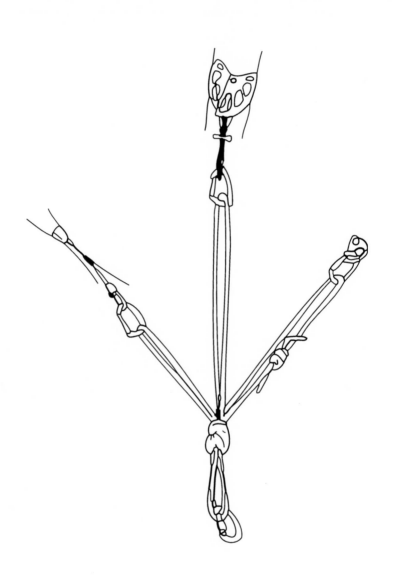

Solid:

An **anchored**man only anchors himself to the Solid Rock.

Solid...As a Rock?

The sun was getting low on the horizon, creating an amber glow on the majestic face of Half Dome across Yosemite Valley. It was the end of a long summer day, and Kevin and Tim were nearing the top of a 400-foot ascent of a spectacular rock climb. Kevin had chosen this intermediate-level climb to prepare Tim for some of the larger "big wall" routes. It was a perfect warm-up for their weekend trip to this rock climbers' paradise.

"Why don't you take the lead on this last part, Tim?" Kevin prodded, as he removed the sling of climbing gear from around his neck and handed it off.

Tim glanced over his shoulder at the treetops far below and asked with cautious excitement, *"You think I'm ready, bro?"*

Peering over the top of the guidebook, Kevin replied, *"Yeah, this pitch is only rated at 5.6 - piece of cake! Speaking of cake, the sooner you get going, the sooner we'll be off this cliff and eating something other than the energy bars you brought. What are these things made of anyway, birdseed and tree sap?"*

Tim double-checked his harness and they exchanged the standard climbing commands:

"On belay?"

   "Belay on."

"Climbing!"

   "Climb on!"

As Tim started climbing up the crack that split the crystal-strewn granite, he felt a sense of exhilaration and surprising confidence. Over the past few weeks he had been learning "trad" climbing, a method where the leader places pieces of gear called "cams" into the rock's cracks as he climbs. The climber then attaches his rope to them using a carabiner, which keeps him connected to the cliff in case of a fall.

Cams

Short for camming units. A handheld mechanical device which uses spring-loaded cam lobes to create opposing force in a crack. These small, yet incredibly strong, pieces of gear have largely replaced pitons for protecting climbers.

Tim found the climbing straightforward, so he only placed a couple of cams as he clawed up the route. Within just a few minutes, he reached the next ledge. His forearms were pumped with blood, and salty sweat dripped into his eyes. He took three more camming units from his gear rack and quickly began to build an anchor. He carefully placed each one behind a single large flake of granite that jutted out from the cliff just a few feet above his head. He gave a quick tug on the anchor before clipping his harness into the carabiner. A sense of accomplishment, and a feeling of relief, welled up inside as he shouted down to his partner, *"Off belay!"*

After giving Kevin the go-ahead signal, Tim leaned back in his harness and started daydreaming about how good the pizza and beer would taste when they got back to the valley floor. A moment later, he heard a loud cracking sound. Before he could react, the large piece of granite he was anchored to broke away from the cliff. He quickly ducked out of the way of the surfboard-sized boulder, but its jagged edge severed the rope as it smashed against the ledge. All at once, Tim and the piece of rock plummeted down the side of the cliff. Kevin watched in horror and disbelief as his friend whizzed by, frantically falling to his death.

Tragically, Tim lost his life because he was anchored to a fragile flake of granite that he assumed would support his body weight. You might think this is a rare, unforeseeable, freak accident. It's not. Every year climbers find themselves tumbling down the sides of mountains because they built an anchor in rock that they assumed was solid. Solid as, well... a rock. Right? Allow me to point out the obvious lesson here: *An anchor is worthless if it is not attached to something solid.*

This leads us to the "S" in our S.R.E.N.E. acronym, which stands for **"Solid." Good anchor systems must be attached to rock that is solid and secure.**

How Long Can You Tread Water?

A few years ago, I was spear fishing off the coast of San Diego. I had recently bought one of those sit-on-top kayaks and loaded it up with my gear. After fighting my way through the breakers, I paddled over to a kelp bed a few hundred yards from the shore. I attached a small anchor to one of the metal hooks on my kayak, and dropped it into the emerald water with a plop. It was time to go looking for some fish.

I spent the next 10 or 15 minutes chasing calico bass in and out of kelp beds. Those little suckers are quick. Right about the time you catch up to one, you're out of breath and you've gotta come back up for air. After many failed attempts, I finally snuck up on an unsuspecting victim. My lungs were already screaming for oxygen when I saw the little fella. Even so, I wasn't going to let this one get away.

"Wait for it...wait for it...now!" I released my spear, which impaled him with a forceful thump, right behind the gills.

There was no time to celebrate the kill. I immediately kicked towards the sunlight with the wriggling fish on the end of my spear. Swimming for the surface with a grin on my face, I was pretty darn proud of myself. "I'm the king of the sea!", I thought. Okay, I was a really-out-of-breath king of the sea who was looking forward to taking a break on his royal kayak.

After what seemed like minutes, I got my first gulp of air. Plain old oxygen never tasted so sweet! Feeling a little light-headed, I took off my foggy mask and began looking for the kayak. I expected it to be a few feet away, but it was nowhere to be found! Feeling concerned, I thought to myself, sarcastically, *"This is not good. Did someone steal it? Was I unknowingly the victim of an open ocean kayak-jacking?"*

After scanning the horizon while treading water, I spotted it. The ocean current had carried it way, way, way down the beach. Apparently it had been giving its puny little anchor a tour of the ocean floor, dragging it through the sand for the last fifteen minutes.

In case you missed it the first time, let me say it again: ***An anchor is only good if it's attached to something solid.***

Life's Most Important Question. Really.

Let's switch gears for a minute. I want to ask you what I believe to be life's most important question: ***What is your life anchored to?***

Think about it for a moment. Do you have something or someone that is kind of like an anchor for your life? If you do, write down who or what it is on the line below.

_____

I believe that every guy's life is anchored to something – even if he doesn't recognize it. Let me run through a few things you may have written down on the line above.

Maybe you wrote down the name of someone you love. Your wife? Girlfriend? Maybe it's your mom or dad, or even your child. Perhaps you've been lucky enough to have a good mentor or coach. As vital and wonderful as these relationships can be, they still fall short. Why? Because even your most trusted friends and family can't be there 100% of the time. They are only human, so they will eventually let you down.

Maybe you've already learned this lesson the hard way. You built your life around the woman you love. You know, the one who according to Jerry Maguire would "complete" you. Then she broke your heart - or left you - because you broke hers. So you pulled up your anchor and reattached it somewhere else. You poured your life into your work. As a result, your identity, ego, and happiness became dependent upon your career.

The harsh reality is that most guys lose a job sometime – and for lots of different reasons. What if your company has to lay you off? What happens if some tech-savvy, just-out-of-high school, snot-nosed computer whiz comes up with an innovation that makes your job obsolete?

Maybe you're still young and cocky enough to think that you don't need anybody else? Perhaps you didn't write anything on the line above, or it's your own name that you wrote on the line. Self-sufficient, huh? Don't need anything or anyone. How's that working out for you? If your answer is, "It's going great," then you should probably just put down this book until you get a little more life experience.

If you think about it long enough, you'll probably come to the same conclusion that I have. All of us are anchored to something. This brings us back to the most important question for you to answer: **What do you want to anchor yourself to?**

Jesus asks the same kind of question, but in a different way: *What is the foundation on which you are building your life?* One day He was talking to a large crowd of His followers who had gathered around to listen to Him teach. He taught them how to build their lives on solid rock:

> **"Therefore everyone who hears these words of mine and puts them into practice is like a wise man who built his house on the rock.**
> **The rain came down, the streams rose, and the winds blew and beat against that house;**
> **yet it did not fall, because it had its foundation on the rock.**
> **But everyone who hears these words of mine and does not put them into practice is like a foolish man who built his house on sand. The rain came down, the streams rose, and the winds blew and beat against that house, and it fell with a great crash."**
> **Matthew 7:24-27**

This is a pretty bold statement for Jesus to make: *Build your life with Me as the foundation or else it will crumble. Anchor yourself to Me.* Seems a bit condescending and self-important, doesn't it? Unless, of course, it's true. Unless He really *is* God. Unless He really *is* the only One who can keep you anchored when life's storms hit.

Making a Run for the Border

I was fresh out of high school and headed south on a surf trip. It was one in the morning as we bumped along the dusty road just outside of Rosarito, Mexico. Four of us were crammed into John's 1987 Toyota FourRunner. The two guys in the back seat were fast asleep. John and I were in the front trying to stay awake. The rear cargo area was stuffed beyond capacity with firewood and camping supplies, with one of those old-fashioned metal ice chests sitting on top. The big, army-green container was packed full of sodas, peanut butter sandwiches, and cheese-filled hot dogs - your standard rations for a surf trip to Baja. On the roof of the vehicle were five or six surfboards, strapped down on racks.

We had left Los Angeles after everyone got off of work, expecting the usual three or four hour trip. Our overly-optimistic goal was to be sitting around a campfire by early evening. After rush-hour traffic,

7-Eleven stops, and a drive through to purchase Mexican auto insurance, it was after midnight when we crossed the border. John and I were blasting '90s grunge rock on his stereo to stay awake. Another hour went by and we turned off the main highway onto the dirt road that would lead to a makeshift campsite.

"Dude, I got an idea," I blurted out. *"Let's get some speed and jump the truck out of the river bed again."*

John and I had been down this same road on our last trip. Right near our campground, it crossed a dried-up river. On our last trip, we passed the time between surf sessions by jumping his truck off of a small dirt ramp leading out of the river bed. The embankments on both sides were fairly gentle slopes. We would drive down one side into the sandy bottom, and then stomp on the gas pedal. As it came up the other side, the vehicle would launch a few feet into the air, "Dukes of Hazzard" style.

Our friends were sleeping soundly in the back seat, probably dreaming about the perfect waves we were hoping to score the next morning. They were completely oblivious as we picked up speed heading toward the jump. *"C'mon, John! Faster! Faster!"* I prodded. *"This is going to be hilarious!"*

John and I cracked up at the thought of them waking up in mid-air! We could see the dip in the road dead ahead. We were probably only going twenty miles an hour, but it felt way faster on this bumpy road. Expecting a smooth drop into the riverbed, John gave it a little more gas.

Smash! The front end of the truck slammed into something and came to a bone-jarring stop. Instantly, the boards flew off the top and over the windshield. The giant metal ice chest came lunging forward, pinning our friend's heads against the back of the front seats. They were definitely awake now!

"Is everyone okay? What happened?" All of us were in shock.

We checked for broken bones and detached body parts, then opened the doors and stepped out. I was so shaken up I didn't notice that the ground was farther away than it should have been. Through dust-filled flashlight beams, we walked around the truck to assess the situation. It was nose down in a ditch, sitting on its twisted frame, with the rear tires a few feet off the ground. Our surfboards lay in the dirt about ten feet away, still attached to the surf racks that were ripped from the roof. We spent the next couple of hours sticking firewood under the back tires, and digging the truck out.

Shift Happens

It had only been a few months since we drove on this road, but since that time, northern Baja had numerous rainstorms. The water run-off had carved a three-foot deep rut in the middle of the riverbed. The last thing I expected when we left on that trip was to be stuck in a ditch in the middle of the night. But that's what happens when storms come. Shift happens. What you thought was solid ground gets washed away. Life gets out of control. You don't know how long it's going to last or how bad it's going to get.

Apparently, we weren't the only ones caught off guard by the storms in Mexico. Just a few miles up the coast was a house that someone had built along the banks of a creek. It was a nice, two-story home with an ocean view, but the builder forgot one little detail - the foundation. They just built it right on the sand. As the water level in the creek rose from the recent storms, it washed the sand right out from under it! I had to snap a photo.

"Honey, did I have too much tequila last night, or has our house become the leaning tower of Baja?"

The Best Decision You'll Ever Make

Jesus warns us that in this life we will have trouble, but to take heart, because He has overcome everything the world can throw at us. He wants to be the foundation upon which you build your life. He wants to be the solid rock to which you anchor your life.

The way you start to build an anchor on Him is by first believing that He is God. He loves you so much that He died for you. When He came to this earth, He lived a sinless life so that He could be a sacrifice to provide forgiveness for your sins. He was killed on a cross to pay the price for everything you have ever done wrong.

God made you, and you're His son. Like any good father, He loves you just because you're His kid. The Bible teaches that God is knocking on the door of your heart. He wants you to open up and invite Him into your life. If you do, He promises to come in and make you a new man, from the inside out.

I have met so many guys who want to believe this, but have no interest in becoming a religious fanatic. They have one foot on the gas, and one on the brake, because they think that following Jesus means you have to be a wimp or a weirdo. Maybe you feel this way, but also know that God has been knocking on the door of your heart. It's no accident that you're reading this book.

I've found that while following Jesus is at times challenging, and often counter-intuitive, it is also very practical and fulfilling. You don't have to check your brain at the door, and you don't have to become an effeminate sweet-guy who prefers choir music to rock 'n' roll. What God does require is that you humble yourself enough to admit you are a sinner, and by faith, ask Him to forgive you. Then, with His help, turn away from your sin. If you are willing to do this, why don't you put your finger in the page and get down on your knees right now. (Unless you're at Starbucks – then maybe you should wait until you're alone.) If you're not sure what to say to God, here's a simple prayer that you can use as a guide:

"God, I want to anchor my life to You. Today I put my faith in You. Please forgive me for everything I've ever done wrong. Jesus, thank you for dying for me. I believe that You are God, and I put my life in Your hands. I need You to be the foundation of my life. I don't want to live for myself anymore. I'm turning the steering wheel of my life over to You. Holy Spirit, please come live inside of me and help me to become the man You want me to be."

If you have prayed this prayer, and meant it from your heart, congratulations! The Bible says you are a new man and that God lives inside of you. He promises to never leave you or forsake you in this life. And as a huge bonus, you'll spend eternity in heaven with Him.

There is no more important decision you can make than to accept this good news of God's love. This is the first and most important step in becoming a man who is anchored to Jesus. **Hebrews 6:19** says, **"We have this hope as an anchor for the soul, firm and secure."** There is no more solid anchor. You can trust your life to Jesus – He's always *bomber!*

Action Step: *If you prayed to make Jesus your Lord, tell someone about the decision you made. Maybe someone gave you this book. If so, give them a call and tell them you've decided to anchor your life to Jesus.*

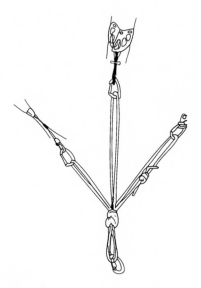

Anchoredman **Principles**

Solid:

An **anchored**man only anchors himself to the Solid Rock.

Redundant:

An **anchored**man employs multiple ways to stay connected to Jesus throughout his week.

We began the last chapter with the story of Tim's fatal fall in Yosemite. His anchor was constructed behind a single flake of fragile granite, which broke away from the cliff. However, a less-than-solid piece of rock was only partly to blame. If Tim had taken the time to attach himself to a nearby tree, or another area of rock, he might have survived. By placing all three cams behind a single piece of rock, he put all his proverbial eggs in one basket.

This leads us to the second climbers' rule and the "R" in our acronym: **"Redundant." Good anchor systems must be constructed of multiple connection points which provide a back up in case one component fails.**

Bumping Into the Woman of Your Dreams

Have you ever gone out of your way to "accidentally" bump into some woman who was really attractive? I can clearly remember the first time I "accidentally" bumped into her. I just happened to show up at school on a day when I didn't have any classes. I lived off-campus, over an hour away, and yet somehow I found myself face-to-face with this stunningly gorgeous sophomore named Corri. To her, it was a chance meeting. No chance. I was on a mission.

It started when one of my life-long friends told me about this "hot chick" who had just moved into the dorms at school. She was a new student at Life Pacific College where all of us went to school. Because I was only taking a couple of classes that semester, I had never met her. But after hearing my friend go on and on for a couple of weeks about how beautiful she was, I had to go see for myself. So I took a vacation day from work and made the seventy-mile commute to attend my school's chapel service that day. Attending chapel was a requirement for all full-time students, so I knew Corri would have to be there.

My plan was to accidentally bump into my buddy's girlfriend, Dawn, who just happened to be roommates with Corri. How lucky. Sure enough, I scored a seat right next to Dawn just before the service started. Even though Corri wasn't with her, I knew I was only one degree of separation away from meeting this mystery girl. While everyone else was singing songs of worship, I was scanning the large auditorium like a sharpshooter to see if I could scope her out. Needless to say, my mind was not on the sermon.

After what seemed like hours, the chapel service finally dismissed. As hundreds of students shuffled their way toward the exits, Dawn said, "Hey Jason, I want you to meet someone."

Hiding my enthusiasm, I complied with a pseudo-surprised look on my face. We then headed over to meet this striking blonde beauty. On the outside, I acted indifferent, but in my head I was quoting Hannibal, George Peppard's character from one of the great television shows of the '80s, *The A-Team*. At the end of each episode, he would light a cigar, and with a cocky grin on his face, say, *"I love it when a plan comes together!"*

A few more steps and there she was, standing right in front of me. My heart started break dancing in my chest. She was mesmerizing. To be honest, I can't remember anything either of us said. I only remember gazing into her brilliant blue eyes and feeling warm all over. With one look, I was enraptured by her beauty. She seemed both out of my league and genuinely approachable. I tried to appear casual and cool, but it was futile.

Even though our "chance" encounter only lasted a few short minutes, it was well worth the two hours of driving time. All the way home, I kept replaying our conversation as I tried, desperately, to recall my mental photos of Corri's kind smile. I couldn't wait to get back to school the next day so I could see her again.

The next day arrived, and I made sure that we *accidentally* bumped into each other several times. In fact, over the next week, I made sure that I would intersect her path enroute to every class. Long story short, we've kept bumping into each other for the last seventeen years. She's my wife, and she is still the girl of my dreams.

Building Connection Points to Jesus

When you're pursuing a relationship with someone, you will go to great lengths to get as much face time with them as possible. If you want to grow closer to someone, you'll find ways to keep bumping into them. The same is true for people who want to grow in their relationship with Jesus. They find ways to bump into God throughout their week. Just like a climber utilizes multiple connection points to anchor themselves to a rock, an *anchoredman* finds ways to stay connected to Jesus throughout his week.

There are many different practices Christians do to grow spiritually. Some people call these practices spiritual disciplines. To me, that sounds too rigid and obligatory. Instead, I like to think of this as finding ways to intentionally bump into Jesus throughout my week. As with any relationship, my walk with God goes through different stages. Sometimes I'm white-hot with passion for spiritual growth. Other times, I feel as spiritually warm as a brass toilet seat on the shady side of an iceberg. Because of this, I've learned to build into my life ways to keep connected to Jesus even if I'm not feeling like it. What follows are five things that are really helpful in my life; they are very doable, regardless of your schedule or spiritual background.

#1 Listen to Worship Music

Music is very powerful. It can motivate you to go faster, or lull you to sleep. It can remind you of your first kiss and bring tears to your eyes. Music can consume your thoughts, especially if you can't get a dumb song out of your head. Case in point: *867-530-niy-ee-ay-eene*. Thanks to Tommy Tutone, Jenny's phone number will be likely bouncing around your noggin for the next few hours! It's funny how the sound of a catchy melody, mixed with a rhythmic beat, can move us. Watching a big-bellied baby, spontaneously dancing around in a soggy diaper, makes it clear that God built us to respond to music. Throw in some meaningful lyrics, and music can even shape your worldview.

I'm a music addict. I don't like doing anything without a soundtrack. I currently have 3,652 songs in my iTunes library, which I have collected over the past twenty years. That, by the way, is after I recently deleted much of my music to make more room on my hard drive. I scaled back and kept only the music I cannot live without.

Among many other genres, I own a lot of worship music. I'm just not talking about music by Christian artists with inspirational lyrics, but more specifically, the kind of songs you'd sing at church. Many of the lyrics in these songs contain phrases from the Bible, or even quote whole verses of Scripture. You can sing these songs as a prayer to God. They can inspire you to spend time with Him. They can remind you of how much He loves you. They can soften your heart, focus your attention, and draw you close to God.

If you don't have any worship music on your iPod, get some. If you don't have an iPod (or another mp3 player), it's time to put down the big magnifying glass you use for reading, throw out your eight tracks, and drive the Buick LeSabre down to Walmart to get one. When you get home, download some new tunes. If you need some suggestions, visit the **"tools"** section at **anchored**man**.com** for a list of some of my favorite worship music. I listen to a wide variety of worship, from '70s classic-rock worship of the "Jesus

Movement" hippies, to the cutting edge, pop-rock worship teams of international mega-churches, to hip hop and Gospel choirs led by charismatic preachers-turned-hype men!

The great thing about music is that, thanks to Steve Jobs, you can listen to it almost anywhere. When you exercise, make it a spiritual workout as well. Getting dressed for the day? Driving to work? Sitting at your desk? Just push play. Get some God-songs into your head and heart. Sing along as if God is listening to you. He is.

One of my favorite things to do is to take a nap with headphones while listening to a worship mix. Even if I don't fall asleep, I'm filled with peace and get rest for my soul.

If you have a family, become a worshipping family. When your kids go to sleep at night, put on some worship music to set a peaceful tone in their room and help them fall asleep to Scripture. I could go on and on, but it really comes down to finding some worship music that inspires you to draw closer to God, and then choose to play it often.

#2 Take a Walk with Jesus

Have you ever heard of a "prayer closet?" Apparently, it's a serene place that really spiritual people have set aside in their home for the purpose of quiet reflection and prayer. Good for them. It doesn't work for me.

I wish I had the ability to sit still for hours and pray. I've always respected people who could. For some reason, I have rarely found much success connecting with God in that way. I either fall asleep or start daydreaming about becoming a quarterback in the NFL, and single-handedly restoring the Oakland Raiders to their long-forgotten glory. One morning I got up early to pray, fell asleep on my Bible, and drooled all over Romans chapter three.

By far, the best way for me to pray interactively with God has been to take walks with Jesus. I have been blessed to live near the ocean for most of my adult life. Over the past decade, Jesus and I have walked almost every mile of coastline in San Diego County together. We've had long, deep conversations about life, love, work, friends, my marriage and four kids. I've been transparent about my fears and insecurities, confessed my sins with blatant honesty, and desperately sought His wisdom to face the problems in my life. Sometimes I just ramble. Sometimes I end up laughing and sometimes I end up crying. I always come away feeling encouraged, connected, and confident that He's proud to be my Dad.

If you've found it hard to develop a regular time of praying, other than a quick *"Thanks, God, for my Double-Western Cheeseburger,"* then try this: Set aside a half hour and pick a place to take a walk where you'll not likely be distracted by other people. Go through the following exercise:

First 10 minutes: Listen to some *worship* music while you walk to focus your attention on God.

Next 10 minutes: Start talking to Jesus (out loud) as if He were walking right next to you. If you're not sure where to start, *thank Him* for what He has done in your life. Then *confess your sins*, and ask Him to forgive you for anything you've done wrong lately. Lastly, *ask for His help* with any challenges you are facing - at work, home, financially, etc. Pray for your friends, family, or even Aunt Susie's cat who has feline diabetes. Cast all your worries on Him; no request is too small or too big.

Last 10 minutes: Ask God: *"What do you want to talk about?"* Then respond by praying about anything He brings to mind. But mostly, just listen. It might take some time, but eventually you will learn to recognize God's voice.

#3 Life Journaling with the Bible

For many people, the most important way to grow spiritually is also the most challenging: studying and living out the Bible. In **Matthew 4:4**, Jesus said, **"Man does not live on bread alone, but on every word that comes from the mouth of God."** He is affirming a foundational truth taught in Scripture. God created humans to need spiritual nourishment. As much as we need food for our bodies, we need food for our soul.

I like this old story about a very poor farmer and his donkey. The farmer had only one animal, a donkey, which pulled his plow in the fields every day. When hard times hit, he could hardly afford the hay to feed it. To make the hay supply last longer, he fed the donkey only half of its regular portion. Because the donkey was both hungry and stubborn, it refused to pull the plow.

The farmer came up with an idea. The next day, he mixed the donkey's hay with some of the inexpensive straw he used for its bedding. The straw had no nutritional value, but at least the donkey would feel full. The farmer was very proud of himself for coming up with a solution. The donkey didn't notice the difference, so the farmer kept giving it a mix of hay and straw.

Months went by and times got harder. To save more money, the farmer kept reducing the amount of good hay in the mixture. He eventually began to give the donkey only small amounts of hay primarily mixed with the empty calories of inexpensive straw. The farmer didn't notice how much weight the donkey was losing until one day it fell over dead while plowing the fields. Even though the donkey felt full, it was suffering from malnutrition. Don't grab your phone and start dialing the number for PETA; it's not a true story. But here's the lesson: *Don't be this donkey!*

Many guys fill their week with activities to keep their plates full: work, family time, television, sports, television, video games, and television. They feel full, but they aren't getting the spiritual nourishment that God created our spirits to need. They lack the spiritual sustenance that can only be found in God's Word. Maybe they go to church once a week to get "fed." Our bodies don't live off of one meal a week; neither do our spirits thrive from simply attending church once a week. Guys who want to grow spiritually aren't satisfied being spoon-fed once a week. They learn to feed themselves from the Bible on a regular basis.

Years ago, I was introduced to a simple and effective spiritual, self-feeding concept developed by a pastor from Hawaii named Wayne Cordeiro. It's called Life Journaling. The idea is to take some time every day to read a passage of Scripture, and then respond to what God shows you by writing it in a journal. When I first heard about Life Journaling, I was skeptical. After a while, I kept bumping into people who said that it changed their lives because it made Bible study so simple and practical. So I decided to give it a try, and wow, it made Bible reading so much more alive!

Using my Life Journal, I began to interact with the Bible in a fresh and relevant way. I found that God used the Bible to give me encouragement, instruction, and wisdom. It's the easiest way I know of to start studying the Bible, even if you don't have a lot of Bible knowledge. You follow the acronym **S.O.A.P.,** which stands for **Scripture, Observation, Application** and **Prayer**.

You can easily create your own journal or visit **www.lifejournal.cc** and purchase one. At this website, you'll find everything you need to get started, including step-by-step instructions for how to journal. If Bible study is new to you, I suggest starting by reading just one chapter a day. Begin with the book of James, then move on to the Gospel of John. On the next page is a sample entry from a Life Journal to help give you an idea of how it works.

date *11.01.10*   title *Be the Tree*

Psalm 1:3 He is like a tree planted by streams of water, which yields its fruit in season and whose leaf does not wither. Whatever he does prospers.

A person who meditates on God's Word will prosper in everything he or she does. People who read the Bible are like strong and healthy trees that get nutrition from rich and moist soil along the banks of a stream.

If I make daily Bible study part of my life, I'll grow spiritually healthy and strong. This is the key to developing a strong spiritual root system for my life. Just like a tree needs deep roots, I need to grow deeper in my relationship with God. Even through the different seasons of life I will prosper if I make time to meditate on God's Word every day.

God you know how busy my life is. You know how I can easily go for days without spending time in the Bible and in prayer. I don't want to just depend on my own strength and wisdom anymore. Please help me develop a habit of reading and memorizing Scripture daily. Holy Spirit speak to me from your Word and help me to understand what I'm reading. I want to obey You and live out the things I learn from Your Word. Thank you for loving me and changing my life. - I love you, Bruce

The Bible teaches that true prosperity and success comes when we read and live out His Word. **Joshua 1:8** says, **"Do not let this Book of the Law depart from your mouth; meditate on it day and night, so that you may be careful to do everything written in it. Then you will be prosperous and successful."** I can't tell you how true this has been in my life. When I study and obey what the Bible teaches, my life just goes so much better.

I know what some of you are thinking: "I've tried it. I don't get it. It's huge, it's old, and it's hard to understand." You're right. The Bible doesn't read as easily as a novel or present its principles in a simple-to-read format like many popular self-help books. It takes more effort. But it's worth it.

Be sure you get a translation that is in everyday English, like the New International Version or New Living Translation. The number one reason people don't read the Bible is because they don't understand it. This leads us to another way to bump into Jesus that helps solve this dilemma.

#4 Listen to Sermon Podcasts

If you want to knock some strokes off your golf handicap, and you're serious about it, you'll pay for some lessons. If you want to understand the Bible better, you will enlist the help of others who can teach you. I've found that the easiest way to do this is by downloading sermons from respected pastors and Bible teachers. Many churches either podcast their services or allow people to download sermons free from their website. My weekly messages are offered at **daybreakchurch.org**. If you're not sure who to listen to, ask your pastor or a trusted spiritual leader for some references. It's rare that a week goes by when I don't bump into Jesus by listening to a message from another pastor.

#5 Find a Good Church and Volunteer

It's 7:46 A.M. on Sunday. You planned to go to church, but...

...there's a crucial game on TV, and your team needs you to be cheering them on through the screen.

...the lawn is so overgrown in the backyard that you haven't seen your dog in weeks.

...you've had a hard week and need rest.

You roll over and pull the pillow over your head. Then you remember that you signed up to volunteer at church this morning. You get out of bed and stumble over to grab your phone from on top of the dresser. You can just call in and give a heads up that you won't be making it to church. As you start to dial the number, you get a whiff of the coffee your wife is brewing downstairs and perk up. You put down the phone. An hour later, you find yourself reluctantly pulling into the church parking lot to keep your commitment because you're a man of your word.

Even though you didn't want to go to church, you went because you didn't want to flake out on your responsibility.

Fast-forward two hours. You leave church feeling glad that you went. The message seemed to be speaking to your life and inspired you to be a better man. After service, you bump into a guy who works in the same building as you. He seems cool. You're going to grab lunch next Tuesday. Now you are going into the start of a new week feeling closer to God.

I've heard it said that women only need one reason to go to church; men need one reason not to go. For many guys, what keeps them coming, week after week, is having a job to do when they get there. That way, even if they don't feel like attending for themselves, they go to fulfill a commitment. When they are done, they're glad they went.

Anchoring yourself to Jesus doesn't happen simply by attending a church service once a week. However, it's a really important part of spiritual growth. **Hebrews 10:25** challenges Christians, **"Let us not give up meeting together, as some are in the habit of doing, but let us encourage one another..."** God wants us to be an active part of a church family. He wants us to spend the first day of the week worshipping Him and being encouraged by other people who are heading in the same direction.

If you are going to a church that you never look forward to attending, you should probably find another one. Even if you have to drive a little, a church alive is worth the drive. While there are no perfect churches, there are great churches all over – you may just have to search for one that fits.

Action Step: *Becoming the leader and protector you want to be happens when you intentionally find ways to bump into Jesus throughout your week. Just like building a redundant anchor requires utilizing multiple connection points, you'll need to find a few different ways to connect yourself to Christ.*

Start now! Don't wait! Begin building your anchor today. On the next page is a checklist for you to accomplish this week: Tear it out of the book and put it in your Bible or on the fridge (whichever you open more) until every box is checked off.

Anchoredman **Checklist**

☐ Download some worship music and put it on your iPod or iPhone, burn some CDs, or make cassettes... however you will use it most.

☐ Take a walk with Jesus sometime today. Use the 10/10/10 format described in this chapter. Don't go to bed until you do this. Even if your walk is a midnight stroll, it will be worth it.

☐ Order a Life Journal or make your own and use the S.O.A.P. method. Start reading the Bible in the book of James. You'll get through the whole book in five days and you'll understand every part.

☐ Pick one or two pastors who podcast. Listen to a sermon while you're in the car or on a jog.

☐ If you don't have one already, find a Christian church that teaches the Bible and one that you'll look forward to attending. Many churches have websites which can help determine if it's a good fit for you.

☐ Once you commit to attend a specific church, find out where they need help. Tell them you're willing to be an usher, work with kids, or go wherever they can use you. Don't check off this box until you are given a weekly task.

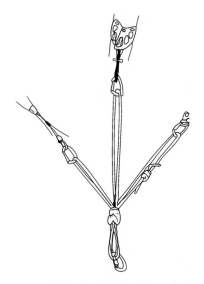

Anchoredman Principles

Solid:

An **anchored**man only anchors himself to the Solid Rock.

Redundant:

An **anchored**man employs multiple ways to stay connected to Jesus throughout his week.

Equalized:
An **anchored**man has close, godly friends to help share the load.

A Frozen Boy Scout Torpedo

On a chilly New Year's Day in 1975, a troop of Boy Scouts were slipping and sliding around on top of the frozen Merced River in Yosemite National Park. Everything about the snowy scene appeared harmless-carefree boys goofing off in a winter wonderland. They seemed totally unaware that a waterfall, which dumped the entire river that was flowing under their feet into thin air, was located just yards downstream of where they were playing. The majestic, 317-foot Vernal Fall has sent its fair share of tourists plunging onto the huge rocks below. Sadly, no one who has gone over Vernal has lived to tell about it.

Chris Becker, an employee at Yosemite's hospital, describes the scene he encountered while hiking: *"The Mist Trail had a bazillion icicles draped across it. At the top of the falls, with the exception of the last twenty feet from the lip, the Merced River was frozen. We had stopped for a breather. I heard a crack like a dish breaking. I looked up and saw one of the kids fall through the ice."*[1]

Instantly, the young Boy Scout flowed under the frozen surface as the forceful current carried him quickly downstream. He was wearing an orange parka, which made him look like a tangerine torpedo zooming along under the semi-transparent ice. There was no air under the ice, which stretched from bank to bank. And yet, not being able to breathe was the least of this kid's problems. Within seconds, he would be airborne and plummeting towards his tragic end. He would have only a second or two to escape the river after clearing the ice. No one could swim to the side in such a short time.

When Becker and his friends arrived to take a break, they stayed on the safe side of the guardrail, and did not have time to make an effort at rescuing the boy. However, one of the adult troop leaders had been standing downstream of the broken ice, and much closer to the waterfall. Likely out of instinct, the man jumped into action. Selflessly, some would say foolishly, he ran toward the perilous lip. Sliding to a stop, he knelt down, and with a perfectly timed lunge of the arm, grabbed the boy's hood as he shot out from under the ice. Next, he heroically pulled the terrified, waterlogged kid back onto the frozen surface. When they pulled his pants off in order to dry him, they froze upright in less than a minute. This unnamed Boy Scout was glad that someone cared enough to pull him back before the icy waters launched him over the cliff.

Every guy needs to have men in his life that care enough to run out on thin ice for him. **Ecclesiastes** chapter four says **"Two are better than one, because** they have a good return for their work: If one falls down, his friend can help him up. But pity the man who falls and has no one to help him up!"

The mighty Vernal Fall

Another Sad Story About a Dude Falling to His Death

On July 5, 2009, the climbing world lost one of its greatest icons: John Bachar. While climbing the eighty-foot Dike Wall near Mammoth Lakes, California, he fell to the ground and died later at a nearby hospital.[2] John was undeniably one of the world's most experienced and gifted climbers. He was incredibly fit and had nerves of steel. So, how did this happen? Did his rope break? No. Did his climbing partner make a belaying error? Nope.

John was a pioneer among a fringe group of climbers who don't use ropes. It's called free soloing. No anchors and no partners to belay - just man versus rock. Free soloists are often among the most elite and confident climbers. In my humble opinion, they are also the most foolish.

In his shortened lifetime, John had literally climbed thousands of expert-level routes without the safety of a rope. The cliff that claimed his life was both easy and familiar. In fact, it was so close to his home, he had climbed it nearly a hundred times. No one knows exactly why he fell from this route that was rated far below his ability. Maybe a piece of rock broke off. Maybe he got distracted or his foot slipped. No one knows because no one else was there.

John Bachar climbing without a rope.

In Memory of John Bachar who started climbing here at Stoney Point

When you hear of John's tragic end, you might condemn him as reckless. Why would he risk so much? It seems foolish to go at it alone. Yet many of us guys are free soloing through life. We lack strong friendships with other guys with whom we can be real. We might have friends, but we don't go too deep in our conversations. It's easy to talk sports, swap fishing stories, or pontificate on what's wrong with Washington, but we seldom go much deeper than that.

This is dangerous. When I think back on the guys I've met who have shipwrecked their lives, I see a common thread. They didn't have close, godly friends. This brings us to the "E" of building a S.R.E.N.E. anchor, and the third word that can save your life: "**Equalized.**"

Good anchor systems are built so that the load is shared equally by all of the components, thereby decreasing the chance that any one component will fail. Likewise, an *anchoredman* has close, godly friends to help share the load.

Ecclesiastes 4:12 says it this way, **"Though one may be overpowered, two can defend themselves. A cord of three strands is not quickly broken."**

You need a few guys who can hike alongside of you through life's adventures. They can help pull you back if you stumble off-route. These men will help shoulder your load when things get heavy. They'll also need you to return the favor when their packs get too heavy. This chapter is about finding those guys.

God wired you to have these strong friendships with other guys who bolster you. **Proverbs 27:17** says, **"As iron sharpens iron, so one man sharpens another."** There is something energizing about hanging out with other guys who are also anchored to Jesus. I learned early on that if I want to get better at any sport, I've got to hang out with other guys who are working toward the same thing. This is also true of spiritual growth. If you want to be a leader and protector in your home, you need to hang around some guys who are working at becoming better husbands, dads, and followers of Jesus.

I Dare You to Juggle Some Hot Coals

When I was a teenager, I spent many nights around a fire on surf trips and campouts. When a few guys get together without a TV to watch, they'll come up with some pretty brainless ways to pass the time. On one such trip, a friend suggested the hair-brained idea that we have a hot-coal juggling contest.

He reached into the fire pit and pulled out, with his bare hands, a white-hot coal that had been sitting a few inches from the blaze. As quickly as he grabbed it, he tossed it high into the cool, night air. It left an electric-yellow trail as it made its arc above his head. To our surprise, he caught it on its way down, and held it just long enough to bat it back into the air. We all stared in awe like a bunch of cavemen. *"Oooh, fire!"*

Then some other moron (I think it was me) said, *"Let me try!"* Within minutes, we were all dancing around the fire like a bunch of juggling idiots. We made up tricky moves, like throwing a coal real high, then spinning around a few times before catching it behind our back.

A drunken guy, who was camping nearby, witnessed our shenanigans and came over to give it a try. We tossed him a small, glowing coal. Instead of batting it back into the air, he just let it land in his hand. The alcohol had not only delayed his reaction time, but apparently numbed the pain, since he didn't drop it for a good eight seconds. Consequently, it seared a red blister into the crease between his palm and the base of his middle finger. This led to the brilliant idea of our next trick - "the stall." We'd let the coal land on our hands, then count out loud for a few seconds to prove our manliness: *"One, two, threeeowww!"*

I found that the secret to pulling off a long stall was to use a coal I had been juggling for a while. After a few minutes, a coal would turn from white to black, with just a little orange glow around the edges. If you were caught with one of these cooled-down coals, someone would call you a wuss and tell you to throw it back. When you tossed the black coal back into the pit, it would heat back up. It would start to glow again, but only after it was next to the other white-hot coals for a while.

If you've ever barbequed the old-fashioned way, with charcoal, you know what I'm talking about. There was always that stray briquette that landed away from the pile and consequently never got hot. You'd have to reach under the grill and flick it into the pile or it was of no use.

This is a great picture of what happens when you hang out with other guys who are "on fire" for God. You need some friends who will help turn up the heat on your spiritual life. In time, you'll become a more selfless husband, more loving dad, and a better man. Why? Because your friends determine your direction.

It's Time to Rate Your Buddies

Proverbs 18:24 says, **"A man of many companions may come to ruin, but there is a friend who sticks closer than a brother."**

This little nugget of wisdom encourages you to look for more than just golfing buddies or people who can expand your business network. You need a friend or two who cares about you as much as he cares about himself. This kind of guy loves you enough to tell you the truth when you are screwing up. He cares about you enough to say, "Let's pray, bro," when you're facing tough times. This kind of friend isn't someone you are worried about impressing or offending. He's got your back and he can be trusted. Most importantly, he wants God's best for you. To see if you currently have any friends like this, rate your buddies with the following test.

Write the names of three buddies on the lines below:

_____

_____

_____

Give them each a point for every "yes" answer to the following questions:

1. Are they full-on, committed followers of Jesus?
2. Are they involved in a church on a weekly basis?
3. Do you hang out at least once a month?
4. Do you regularly talk about deep things with them?
5. Do you guys have a common interest, sport or hobby?
6. Have you ever asked them for help or vice versa?
7. Have you ever prayed out loud together?
8. Have you moved past trying to impress them instead of just being yourself?
9. Have you ever had a conflict or argument and then worked through it?
10. Would you trust them to raise your kids in case of an emergency?

If one of your friends scored eight points or more, then you probably have a Proverbs 18:24 friend. This kind of guy is rare. Make sure you buy him Starbucks on a regular basis!

If you answered no to most of the questions, it's either time to find some new buddies, or intentionally deepen some of your friendships. Take the initiative to invite some guy to play a sport that you're both interested in, or just go grab a cup of coffee. Along the way, tell him about what God is doing in your life and see how he responds. You'll know pretty quickly if he's the kind of guy who might become a true brother.

Maybe you can turn a guy who's a five into an eight or nine. I know it sounds a bit like speed dating for a *bro-mance*. Get over it! If you want to stay anchored to Jesus, you can't be a free-soloing Christian. Anchored men have close, godly friends to help share the load.

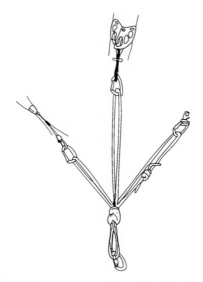

Anchoredman **Principles**

Solid:
An **anchored**man only anchors himself to the Solid Rock.

Redundant:
An **anchored**man employs multiple ways to stay connected to Jesus throughout his week.

Equalized:
An **anchored**man has close, godly friends to help share the load.

No Extension:

An **anchored**man doesn't allow extended periods of time to pass without confessing sin.

Tiger Woods.

Ted Haggard.

Bill Clinton.

I could keep listing names, but unless you're still in the Y2K bunker, you already know what these guys have in common. They made headlines when their secret lives were exposed to the whole world. When we hear about another celebrity, politician, or spiritual leader who is living a double life, we all cringe. For many of us, it's because we can imagine the shameful suffering we would experience if our own secrets were uncovered. Go ahead and think about it. What would happen if your hidden sins were made known to your family, co-workers, and friends? Scary thought, huh?

The Day a Bomb Landed on Our House

I was only ten years old. It was a typical, sunny California, January day. My brothers and I were playing in the front yard, waiting for my parents to return from an overnight trip, when a car came down the street. Through the windshield, I could see my mom in the front seat, but next to her, instead of my dad, was Pastor Jack. Jack Hayford was the pastor of a church in Los Angeles where my family attended church most of my young life. The only reason we weren't still attending his church is because my father had been sent out to be the pastor of a church in nearby Simi Valley. For the past five years, Dad had pastored this growing church in a quaint town that had become our version of Mayberry. That was all about to change.

As my brothers and I followed Pastor Jack and mom into the house, it occurred to me that he wouldn't be here unless something was wrong. We could see it on my mom's face. As they began talking to us in an overly calm tone, I remember thinking to myself, *"Dad is dead! They have come to tell us that we will never see our dad again."* My heart was pounding and my eyes filled with tears.

A few minutes later, Pastor Jack told us that dad had left. He decided to leave my mom to pursue an adulterous relationship with a woman from our church. Even though I didn't really understand what all that meant, I knew that he had done something really bad and probably wasn't coming back. In one day, our lives were turned upside down as my dad's secret life was exposed. We immediately packed up our belongings and drove to Pastor Jack and Anna's house. I never slept in our house again. I never went back to my school. Because my dad was the pastor, I was pulled away from my best friends at church. Worst of all, I couldn't cry on my dad's shoulder because he was the one who had done this to us. Even though it was more than 25 years ago, I can still remember the overwhelming sense of sorrow and abandonment that I felt.

Apparently, my dad had been hiding his sinful relationship with this woman for months. He would preach a sermon on Sunday, and then cheat on my mom during the week. Nobody knew about his secret life until it all came crashing down.

Have you ever wondered how that is possible? How can someone hide something so horrible for so long, knowing that it's going to crush those they love the most when it inevitably comes out? Ask my dad and he'll tell you. It always starts small.

Do Sweat the Small Stuff

My dad didn't wake up one morning and say to himself, *"Today I think I'll leave my wife, abandon my four kids, throw away my life's work at church, and let down everyone in the congregation in exchange for the thrill of a doomed-from-the-start fling with another woman."* Undoubtedly, he started by entertaining seemingly harmless but lustful thoughts in his mind. Those thoughts marinated until he regularly fantasized about what it would be like to act out those perilous and exhilarating mental movies. He would conduct private counseling appointments with this woman, all the while tiptoeing forward, in small increments, with inappropriate flirtations. He saw danger coming, ignored the flashing, warning lights, and kept going.

Someone once said that:
"Sin will take you farther than you want to go,
keep you longer than you want to stay,
and cost you more than you're willing to pay."

God knows the deceptive and progressive nature of sin, so he created a way for us to avoid the secret-sin trap. It's not an easy path, but it's clear:

**"Therefore confess your sins to each other and
pray for each other so that you may be healed.
The prayer of a righteous man is
powerful and effective."
James 5:16**

Go back and read it again. It's God's plan for you to have someone in your life to whom you can regularly confess sin. This is how you avoid the double-life syndrome.

You might be thinking, *"I ain't confessin' nuttin' to nobody!"*

I get it. It takes courage to tell someone about the junk in your life. I know. I have done it many times, and I can tell you, it is never easy. However, when you finally get the guts to do it, and that person prays for you, it's powerful! My greatest victories over sinful habits have come from a Christian brother praying for me after I have confessed my sin to him. That's why I try not to allow long periods of time to go by without confessing my sin first to God, and then to another guy. This leads us to the last two letters of the S.R.E.N.E. acronym. The "N" and "E" stand for **"No Extension."**

Good anchor systems should be constructed without any slack, so that if a component does fail, the remaining components are not shock loaded.

When three pieces of climbing protection are equalized to share the load, it's important that there is no extra slack in the system. Just a few inches of slack can give a falling climber a chance to pick up speed before shock loading the rest of the anchor when it becomes taut.

Imagine you have been tugging on your child's loose tooth, but it won't come out. Tie a piece of string around the tooth, and then tie the other end to a doorknob, allowing the string to sag with a few feet of slack. When you slam the door shut, the slack pulls tight and the tooth goes flying. This works great for a loose tooth, but is the opposite of what you want to happen to your climbing anchor. It's also the opposite of what you want to happen in your life when it comes to confessing sin.

An anchoredman doesn't allow extended periods of time to pass without confessing sin. He knows that we can be blinded by our sin when we fail to apply the "No Extension" principle in our lives.

This is why we shouldn't allow too much time to go by between our times of prayer, confession, and Bible study. We need to keep bumping into Jesus throughout the week. We need some guys in our life who will pray for us and watch out for slack that could be building up in our spiritual anchor system.

In the next few pages, I want to share with you three practices that I believe are critical to avoiding a double life and for keeping slack out of your spiritual anchor system.

#1 Confess Small, Sin Small

There is a great scene in the movie, *The Patriot*, where Mel Gibson's character, Benjamin Martin, is about to ambush the enemy to free his captive son. Benjamin takes his two younger sons to a hill above the road where a stagecoach carrying his oldest son and several British soldiers is about to pass by. He has enlisted his boys, who weren't even teenagers yet, to shoot the soldiers and help free their older brother. As he hands them their rifles, he reminds them of instructions he had given them for hunting:

"Boys, what have I always told you about shooting?"

With wide-eyes, the little soldiers respond in unison, *"Aim small, miss small."*

"That's right, aim small, miss small," he affirms as he heads off to his own perch a few yards away.

As the stagecoach approaches, the youngest son takes aim, while whispering his father's advice to himself once again, *"Aim small, miss small."*

What happens next is a violent musketfest that ends with a bunch of Redcoats getting pumped full of lead, or worse, losing their white-wigged scalps to a maniacal, blood-soaked Gibson. It's awesome! But I digress.

I'd like to give you similar advice for overcoming sin: **Confess small, sin small**. Make it a part of your regular life to confess small transgressions before they grow into the kinds of sins that can bring widespread destruction. It's much easier to confess lustful thoughts to a trusted friend than to confess an adulterous affair to your wife. It's better to confess a little dishonesty to a brother than to stand before a judge for illegal financial dealings.

I wonder what would have happened if my dad had confessed his sinful desires, and received prayer, before he shipwrecked his whole family and church. Telling someone you've sinned takes humility and courage, but it will spare you from more grievous consequences.

#2 Keep No Secret Sins

I've got some bad news. You are never going to live a sinless life. Because you are human, you're going to sin. But you don't have to have *secret* sins. That's your choice.

Proverbs 28:13 says, **"He who conceals his sins does not prosper, but whoever confesses and renounces them finds mercy."**

God doesn't expect you to live a perfect or sinless life. He does, however, want you to have the guts to confess your sins so that you don't lead a double life. You can't hide sin forever. The Bible says that you can be assured that your sins will be exposed. Think about that for a moment. Scary, huh? The good news is that sins lose their power when they aren't hidden in the dark closet of our secret lives. If you have a secret sin, I beg you, summon the courage to tell someone who is a trusted Christian so they can pray for you. You won't regret it.

#3 Keep Stepping Forward

"Tom, you got me?" I yelled out in a panicked voice that was as manly as an eight-year-old soprano from the Vienna Boys' Choir. You can hardly blame me; I was 300 feet up the side of Half Dome and my feet were sliding off the rock. If I fell, there was only a single rope, about as thick as my pinky, separating me from the treetops way below. When you are that high up, a climbing rope feels more like a piece of dental floss!

It was my first climbing trip in Yosemite. My new climbing partner, Tom, offered to lead me up an 800-foot route called *Snake Dike*, on the southwest side of the Dome. It's mostly easy climbing with the exception of a few tricky sections. The most difficult part is a "friction traverse," about 300 feet off the deck.

Tom had warned me about this part. It's a featureless section of rock that requires you to trust the friction of your climbing shoes against smoothly polished granite. Since there are no handholds, you can't grab anything. You have to look for pea-sized rock crystals to stand on and hope for the best. Tom also gave me some great advice right before he led out across the friction section:

"If your feet start sliding off, just keep taking steps."

Those words came back to mind now as I started slipping. You see, my first reaction was to dig my fingernails into the granite and hold my shaking, sweaty body as still as possible. I mistakenly thought this would help me stick to the rock. Nope. Still slipping. Even though it felt counterintuitive, I trusted Tom's advice and took another step. Just as my right foot skated off, my left foot came into contact with the rock. My left foot started slipping, so I then took another step with my right. Slip. Left. Slip. Right. Slip. Left. I was virtually moon walking my way across near vertical rock until I eventually reached my next handhold.

If I had stayed still another few seconds, paralyzed by fear, I would have surely come off the rock and taken the longest fall of my short, climbing career. "Keep taking steps forward" is also great advice for spiritual growth.

If you're like me, your tendency is to stop moving forward when you sin. You don't talk to God about it because, well... God's mad, right? So you separate yourself from Him, maybe stay away from church, isolate yourself from other Christians, and become stuck in your guilt. This only arrests your forward spiritual momentum and causes you to keep slipping farther away.

The Best Defense Is a Good Offense

You've probably heard the old football truism: The best offense is a good defense. This may be true for sports, but I believe the opposite is true for spiritual growth. If we are constantly focused on spiritual defense (e.g., trying to block sin or stop bad habits), we'll never succeed. I've found it far more effective to concentrate on taking steps forward in my relationship with Jesus, and as a result, my sin level goes down. When it comes to conquering sin, I'm convinced that the best defense is a good offense.

To keep taking steps forward, we have to believe God's Word when it says in **1 John 1:9, "If we confess our sins, He is faithful and just and will forgive us our sins and purify us from all unrighteousness."**

Don't let the guilt of sin paralyze you or keep you from approaching God. If you start slipping up, confess your sin, believe God has forgiven you, and take another step forward. God doesn't need a cooling-off period before you can pray after sin - the sooner the better. Don't let slack build up. "No Extension!"

God Is in the Restoration Business

Much like my dad, King David from the Bible had a colossal failure as a leader when he committed adultery with Bathsheba. After experiencing the devastating consequences of his sin, he wrote a poem of humble confession to God. In **Psalm 51**, David wrote:

1 **"Have mercy on me, O God, according to your unfailing love; according to your great compassion blot out my transgressions. *2* Wash away all my iniquity and cleanse me from my sin.**

3 **For I know my transgressions, and my sin is always before me. *4* Against you, you only, have I sinned and done what is evil in your sight, so that you are proved right when you speak and justified when you judge.**

5 Surely I was sinful at birth, sinful from the time my mother conceived me. 6 Surely you desire truth in the inner parts; you teach me wisdom in the inmost place.

7 Cleanse me with hyssop, and I will be clean; wash me, and I will be whiter than snow. 8 Let me hear joy and gladness; let the bones you have crushed rejoice. 9 Hide your face from my sins and blot out all my iniquity.

10 Create in me a pure heart, O God, and renew a steadfast spirit within me. 11 Do not cast me from your presence or take your Holy Spirit from me.

12 Restore to me the joy of your salvation and grant me a willing spirit, to sustain me.

13 Then I will teach transgressors your ways, and sinners will turn back to you. 14 Save me from bloodguilt, O God, the God who saves me, and my tongue will sing of your righteousness.

15 O Lord, open my lips, and my mouth will declare your praise. 16 You do not delight in sacrifice, or I would bring it; you do not take pleasure in burnt offerings.

17 The sacrifices of God are a broken spirit; a broken and contrite heart, O God, you will not despise.

18 In your good pleasure make Zion prosper; build up the walls of Jerusalem. 19 Then there will be righteous sacrifices, whole burnt offerings to delight you; then bulls will be offered on your altar."

I have prayed Psalm 51 countless times as a guide for confessing sin to God. I suggest you do the same. It's a humble and desperate plea for restoration from sin and condemnation. There is a key phrase in verse six that is easy to overlook. **"Surely you desire truth in the inner parts..."** is a reminder that God wants us clean and holy more than we do. When we sin, He longs to forgive us, wash us, and restore us.

Who Needs a GPS When You Can Get Turn-by-Turn Directions from God

I've seen God's desire to restore displayed in miraculous ways throughout my life. My favorite miracle was when God began the restoration process for my dad, after he had committed adultery.

When my dad left my mom for the other woman, he literally hid himself from everyone he knew. He moved out and didn't tell anyone where he was going. After nearly a week, no one had heard from him. God had shown my mother through prayer and Bible study that He was going to restore their marriage and eventually turn this horrible situation around.

My Uncle Bob had heard the same thing from God and decided to start looking for my dad. For all we knew, he could have been in another state or on a plane to Mexico. In 1984, you couldn't track someone electronically through credit card transactions, cell phone bills, etc., so he began to pray for God's help to locate my dad. You're not going to believe what happened next!

After praying, my uncle started driving around, trusting that God would help guide him. He was cruising around Chatsworth, California, like someone looking for a lost dog, when he came across a street called Independence Avenue. God told him to turn down that street. Then, like a supernatural GPS navigation system, God miraculously guided him through a neighborhood, then down another street to an apartment complex. There was my dad's car parked outside! Let this be a reminder: you can't run from God... *or my Uncle Bob!*

Finding my dad was the first step in the long process of restoring my parents' marriage. To make a very long story short, my dad whole-heartedly repented. He asked for forgiveness from my mom, us kids, and the members of the church he used to pastor. For the next few years, he and my mom split their time between intensive marriage counseling and necking in the front seat of the car like Richie Cunningham and Lori Beth at Inspiration Point. *(For those of you born after the seventies, google "Happy Days.")*

My parents are still happily married over 26 years later. They regularly share their story at marriage retreats and even help counsel other couples going through marital crisis. Because my dad was humble enough to confess his sin, enlist the support of other men, and re-anchor himself to God, he turned his life around. Beyond that, he has redeemed the legacy of his life from "home-wrecker" into one of God's great comeback stories.

God still goes to great lengths to heal broken marriages and restore prodigal sons. I've seen Him do miracles to help men, broken by moral failure, become securely anchored to Jesus. Maybe you are in the middle of a painful family crisis. Maybe, like King David, you are experiencing the heartbreaking consequences of your sinfulness. If you are desperate for God to restore you, let me assure you that He can, and will, if you'll let Him.

As I said earlier, it is no accident that you are reading this book right now. God wants to restore hope to your life. He wants you to surrender your life to Him, and lay your burdens at His feet. He will meet you right where you are today.

Action Step: *Go back through Psalm 51 right now. Make David's words your own. Don't let another minute go by without confessing to God. Don't allow any more slack to build up in your anchor. Get on your knees right now and cry out to God. Then follow the advice from this chapter. Confess your sin to a trusted friend so he can pray for you. The prayer of that friend will be powerful and effective!*

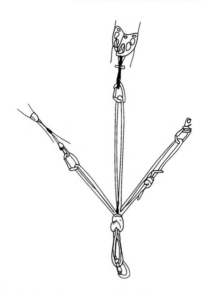

Anchoredman Principles

Solid:
An **anchored**man only anchors himself to the Solid Rock.

Redundant:
An **anchored**man employs multiple ways to stay connected to Jesus throughout his week.

Equalized:
An **anchored**man has close, godly friends to help share the load.

No Extension:
An **anchored**man doesn't allow extended periods of time to pass without confessing sin.

Stay Tied In

He Maintained a Proper Belay

On Sunday, June 13, 1999, Peter Terbush and two friends, Kerry and Joseph, were climbing in cool evening temperatures on Yosemite's Glacier Point Apron. Pete belayed from the ground as Kerry began ascending what looks like a two-thousand-foot-high granite wave. Peter's father, Dr. James Terbush, tells the story of what happened to his son that day...

"Pete and his two friends were climbing a relatively easy rock route below Glacier Point. Pete was the belayer for Kerry. Pete held the rope which was run through several nuts, slings and carabiners and would support Kerry, if he was to fall. Kerry was a full rope length, about 160 feet, above Peter. Joe was at the base of the climb with Pete.

"A large section of granite rock, approximately 200 tons, loosened by repeated cycles of freezing and thawing and expansion of cracks, came loose a thousand or so feet above the climbers. As rocks and boulders the size of Volkswagens began tumbling down a rock chute, Joe took cover away from the exploding rocks. The place where Joe was sitting, and where his sweater remains, is covered with a huge boulder. Rock shrapnel was everywhere.

"Pete, as belayer, pulled into the arrest position expecting Kerry to fall. He leaned into the slope, but did not flee to the cover of a nearby protecting boulder. He could easily have done so, even tripped into the space behind a boulder, but would have lost control of the belay. The noise was deafening. Granite dust filled the valley, causing tourists to flee in horror.

"When the rocks stopped falling, the young men began calling to each other through the dust. Joe found Peter, still in the arrest position holding the rope attached to Kerry above. He had been killed by the rock shrapnel from a falling boulder. Pete's hands were fixed and in position, his left hand on the rope above and his right pulled down hard against his right hip loading the rope into the arresting device fixed to the harness at his waist. Kerry yelled at Joe to go get help for Pete, but Joe could tell Pete had been killed instantly. In order to get Kerry down, Joe had to pry the rope from Peter's hands, which remained fixed.

"Yosemite Park Search and Rescue could not get Pete's body down for another 24 hours due to the risk of rock fall. Joe and Kerry both had injuries from rock shrapnel that required suturing. Both young men are adamant that Pete saved Kerry's

life. He stood there like a rock and took it. He was a rock.

"He was Peter, 'the rock.'"[3]

Peter was twenty-one years old when he sacrificed his life to make sure his friend wouldn't lose his. Between a carabiner and his belay device, these five words are engraved on Peter's tombstone: *"He maintained a proper belay."* These words don't mean much to many people. To a rock climber, they mean the difference between life and death.

Also engraved on Peter's tombstone is a Bible verse: **"Greater love has no one than this, that he lay down his life for his friends." John 15:13**

Jesus is the one who spoke these words. Then He laid down his own life for you. He didn't have to. He could have gotten down from the cross. With just a word, He could have struck dead those who arrested Him. He could have stayed in Heaven and let you pay the price for your own sins. But He loves you too much. He really does. He proved it when He chose to subject Himself to a bloody, violent form of execution so that you could be forgiven - His life for yours. His death and resurrection make it possible for sinful people like us to have a personal relationship with our holy God.

Staying Tied In

As you read **John 15:1-11**, keep an eye out for the word that Jesus uses eleven times.

1 **"I am the true vine, and my Father is the gardener.** *2* **He cuts off every branch in me that bears no fruit, while every branch that does bear fruit he prunes so that it will be even more fruitful.** *3* **You are already clean because of the word I have spoken to you.** *4* **Remain in me, and I will remain in you. No branch can bear fruit by itself; it must remain in the** vine. Neither can you bear fruit unless you remain in me.

5 "I am the vine; you are the branches. If a man remains in me and I in him, he will bear much fruit; apart from me you can do nothing. *6* If anyone does not remain in me, he is like a branch that is thrown away and withers; such branches are picked up, thrown into the fire and burned. *7* If you remain in me and my words remain in you, ask whatever you wish, and it will be given you. *8* This is to my Father's glory, that you bear much fruit, showing yourselves to be my disciples.

9 "As the Father has loved me, so have I loved you. Now remain in my love. *10* If you obey my commands, you will remain in my love, just as I have obeyed my Father's commands and remain in his love. *11* I have told you this so that my joy may be in you and that your joy may be complete."

Did you get it? Go back through this passage and every time you see the word "remain," circle it. What do you think Jesus is trying to drill into our noggins? He knows how easy it is for us to disconnect ourselves from Him. In this busy world we live in, it is hard for us to unplug from all of the electronic gadgets to which we seem to be tethered. Some guys won't even sit on the porcelain throne without their iPhone. Sadly, it seems so much easier for us to unplug from God.

It might surprise you to know that many climbing injuries and deaths are caused by climbers deliberately disconnecting themselves from their rope. Maybe they are on a ledge where it seems safe to walk around. Maybe they get to the top of a climb and feel a false sense of security from all of the adrenaline pumping through their system. For one reason or another, they unclip a carabiner, or untie the rope from their harness. Now it takes just one small slip, and it's a one-way ticket to "groundsville" on the express elevator. This is precisely why many climbing videos and books end with the same advice: "Always stay tied in to the rope."

This is the advice I'd like to drill into your head as you finish this book. Always stay tied in! You have a God who has promised that He will never disconnect Himself from you. Jesus gave His life to make sure you could be permanently anchored to Him. He isn't going to drop you when times get tough, or take you off belay because you have sinned too much lately. In **Hebrews 13:5**, God has said, **"Never will I leave you; never will I forsake you."** If you find yourself feeling disconnected from Him, it's because you didn't stay tied in.

It's like the old married couple driving down a country road in their 1957 Ford pickup. Betty, who is sitting in the passenger seat, starts crying. When Fred asks her what's wrong, she sniffles, *"I just realized we don't sit close anymore."*

    "What do you mean, Betty?" asks Fred.

    "We used to cuddle up next to each other when we drove around town. Now I sit here and you sit way over there. Look at how much seat there is between us."

    Fred looks down at the steering wheel, then over to Betty and says, *"Well, I didn't move!"*

    If you are feeling far from God, it's not because He has moved away from you. It's because you have slid away from Him. Scoot over.

Tied In, Not Tied Down

    Some would say that freedom means not being tethered to anything or anyone. Yet I've found that in some cases, the exact opposite is true. When climbing, being tied in allows me to experience places I'd never get to without the safety of a rope. Have you ever watched a spectacular sunset while perched on an eighteen-inch ledge, hundreds of feet up the side of a granite wall? It is breathtaking. Have you ever run back and forth across a vertical cliff, like the pendulum from a thousand-foot-high grandfather clock? It feels exhilarating, terrifying, and freeing, all at the same time!

Staying tied in to God doesn't mean being tied down. On the contrary, being anchored to God almost guarantees that your life is going to be an adventure.

Look at the lives of guys in the Bible who were serious about following God and you'll see that they were anything but bored. Some of them brawled with ferocious lions and decapitated giants. Some fought bloody battles against vicious enemies. Some ate bugs while living in the wilderness and others survived violent storms at sea. These guys could be Randy Couture's fight coach and make Bear Grylls seem "indoorsy."

I'm so sick of hearing guys say that being a Christian means you'll have to settle for a boring life. They don't know what they're talking about. I recently met with a friend who followed God's prompting to make Christian surf flicks. Over breakfast, he enthralled me with the story of his most recent surf trip to South Africa:

"Last year I found myself hanging out of a helicopter while filming Tom Curren rip up Jeffreys Bay. I just thought to myself, 'I can't believe where God has taken me. I'd never be here if I didn't obey God!'"

For those of you who aren't familiar with pro-surfing, this would be like playing a round with Tiger at

Pebble Beach or riding shotgun with Dale Earnhardt, Jr. at Daytona. Though I've yet to surf J-Bay, I could relate to my friend's feelings of awe and gratitude.

I love the freedom and adventure that comes from being tied in to God. I love that He is faithful, but not predictable. He is dangerous and trustworthy at the same time. I've learned that I can be in a risky situation and still feel totally secure because I'm anchored to Jesus. I've learned that His plans for me are far bigger and scarier than my own. I've learned that when He says "no" or "wait," it's only because He's got something planned that's way, way, way better.

The Bible says that God doesn't withhold anything that's good for us, and that every good and perfect gift comes from Him. Jesus said He came so we can have life to the fullest, and experience true and lasting freedom. There's no way I'm anchoring myself to anyone or anything else!

I'm staying tied in for life.
How about you?

Notes

Chapter 3: Equalized

1. Michael P. Ghiglieri and Charles R. "Butch" Farabee, Jr., *Off the Wall: Death in Yosemite* (Puma Press, 2007), 22.

2. Luke Laeser, *John Bachar 1957-2009*, (Climbing.com), Photo by Phil Bard

Chapter 5: Stay Tied In

3. The Peter Terbush Story, (Solid Rock Climbers for Christ), srcfc.org

Acknowledgements

Jesus, for being the anchor of my life. I'm so thankful that I've never known a day without Your love and presence.

Corri, for being my best friend and the love of my life. Everything you do for me and the kids will surely earn you a huge mansion in heaven - hopefully with two washing machines.

Bubba, Mookie, Bu and Berry. You are always the brightest part of my day.

Dad and Mom, (Graves, Wymore and Scott) for your constant love, and never making us kids wonder if you are proud of us. How blessed we are to have anchored parents.

Gary Webb, for being a true Proverbs 18:24 friend. Whenever you get involved in anything, you make it better.

Ryer Flaker, for working hard on the book and website for less than minimum wage. Your artwork is extraordinary.

Lynette Trier, Dick Scott, Julie Brierley, Jim Ford, Tom Chapin, Tom Skawski, Calvin Landrus, and anyone else who helped give feedback and kept this project moving forward.

The *anchoredmen* of Daybreak Church. This book was written for you guys.

About the Author

Jason Graves is a native Southern Californian who loves living in north San Diego County with his wife, Corri, and their four children: Benjamin, Cameron, Annelise, and Ella.

He currently serves as lead pastor at Daybreak Church in Carlsbad, California. Jason and his wife have been married for 15 years and have served together in ministry since they were dating. In his free time, Jason enjoys surfing, rock climbing and listening to loud music - loudly. He also enjoys leading climbing and backpacking adventures for guys who are interested in becoming godly leaders.

Want Jason to speak at your church or men's event?

For more information or to inquire about speaking engagements, please send an email to **info@anchoredman.com.**

CPSIA information can be obtained at www.ICGtesting.com
Printed in the USA
BVOW01s0146060514

352247BV00001B/8/P